FABULOUS ANIMALS

The Story of the Komodo Dragon

Anita Ganeri

capstone

To contact Capstone Global Library please call 800-747-4992, or visit our web site www.mycapstone.com

Edited by Linda Staniford
Designed by Philippa Jenkins
Original illustrations © Capstone Global Library Limited 2016
Picture research by Morgan Walters
Production by Victoria Fitzgerald
Originated by Capstone Global Library Ltd
Printed and bound in China

19 18 17 16 15
10 9 8 7 6 5 4 3 2 1

Library of Congress Cataloging-in-Publication Data
Cataloging-in-publication information is on file with the Library of Congress.
Written by Anita Ganeri
ISBN 978-1-4846-2711-2 (hardcover)
ISBN 978-1-4846-2715-0 (paperback)
ISBN 978-1-4846-2719-8 (eBook PDF)

Acknowledgments
The author and publisher are grateful to the following for permission to reproduce copyright material: Alamy: epa european pressphoto agency b.v., 23, Joe Quinn, 7, Prisma Bildagentur AG, Cover, Stocktrek Images, Inc., 27; Bryan Fry, 26; Corbis: Natalie Fobes/Science Faction, 22; Dreamstime: Conny Fuchs, 4, Edmund Lowe, 25; iStockphoto: Andrew Conway, 10, EdStock, 20, NI QIN, 9; Jeri Imansyah, 21; Minden Pictures: Michael Pitts, 19; Newscom: Hasyim Widhiarto/picture alliance/ANN/The Jakar, 11, Marko König imageBROKER, (dragon) top 15, RKO/Album, 6; Shutterstock: Anna Kucherova, 5, Edmund Lowe Photography, 14, h4nk, 8, john michael evan potter, 16, KayaMe, (lizard) left 15, Matt Jeppson, 12, Soren Egeberg Photography, 13, Vladimir Wrangel, 24; SuperStock: Cyril Ruoso / Minden Pictures, 17, Minden Pictures, 18.

We would like to thank Michael Bright for his invaluable help in the preparation of this book.

007485LEOS16

Contents

Some words are shown in bold, like this. You can find out what they mean by looking in the glossary.

Dragon Search

For hundreds of years, sailors told stories about huge "dragons" living on a few tiny islands in Indonesia. In 1910, a Dutch soldier led an expedition to Komodo Island. He wanted to see these amazing creatures for himself.

This is Komodo Island in Indonesia.

Was this animal a dragon?

The soldier killed one of the creatures. He sent the skin and some photos to a scientist. The scientist worked at Bogor Zoo on the nearby island of Java. He sent out another expedition to catch some young live dragons for the zoo.

Stories spread quickly about the strange creatures. They became known as Komodo dragons. In 1926, an American explorer named W. Douglas Burden set off for Komodo Island. He wanted to catch a live dragon to take back to the United States.

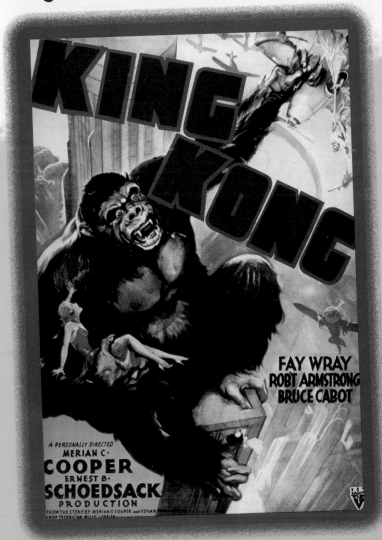

The film *King Kong* was based on Burden's expedition.

These stuffed dragons are on display in a museum.

Burden reached the island. He headed into the forest and put out some meat as **bait**. Then he waited for a Komodo dragon to come. He did not have to wait for long. In total, Burden brought back two live dragons and 12 dragon skins.

Dragon Tales

But was this amazing animal *really* a dragon? For centuries, people in Asia had told stories about dragons. Like a Komodo dragon, these creatures had huge, scaly bodies and hatched from eggs. Dragons were thought to bring good luck.

In China, dragons like this one were lucky.

Dragons were said to have large teeth.

In some places, people dug up ancient fossil teeth in their fields. They thought that these were dragons' teeth. People believed that the teeth had magical powers. They ground them up and used them to make medicines.

Local people already knew all about Komodo dragons, long before the Europeans came. They believed that the dragons were their **ancestors**. They treated them with great **respect**.

This is a local village on Komodo Island.

Dragons sometimes come into villages.

If local hunters killed a deer
or goat, they left out half of
the meat for the dragons to eat.
They do not do this anymore. If a dragon
comes into the village, they do not harm or
kill it. They shout and shoo it away.

Meet the Komodo Dragon

Scientists studied the skins and live animals that Burden brought back. They figured out that the Komodo dragon was actually a huge **reptile**. Reptiles are a group of animals that includes snakes and crocodiles.

Snakes are reptiles, like Komodo dragons.

A Komodo dragon smells with its tongue.

The Komodo dragon is a **monitor lizard**. It has scaly, brown skin. It has a tail as long as its body. It has a long, **forked** tongue. It flicks its tongue in and out to pick up the smell of its **prey**.

Dragon Lifestyle

Wild Komodo dragons only live in Indonesia in southeastern Asia. They are found on Komodo Island and some other small islands nearby.

This is Rinca Island, part of the Komodo dragons' home.

feet

0 1 2 3 4 5 6 7 8 9 10

A green lizard is
6 inches
(15 centimeters) long.

Komodo dragons
are huge lizards.

A Komodo dragon can grow up to
10 feet (3 meters) long. It can weigh
as much as an adult human. It is the
biggest and heaviest lizard in the world.
It is also very strong and powerfully built.

Komodo dragons are meat-eaters.
They mostly eat dead animals, but
they also go hunting for food. They can
knock down a wild pig or deer with a
swipe of their strong tails.

Komodo dragons
also hunt
water buffalo.

These Komodo
dragons are
eating their prey.

A Komodo dragon has sharp, **serrated** teeth. It holds its **prey** in its front legs. Then it tears off big chunks of meat and swallows them whole. It can eat three-quarters of its own weight in one meal.

In September, the female dragon digs a hole in the ground for a nest. The female lays around 30 eggs. She lies on the nest to keep the eggs warm.

A Komodo dragon looks out of its nest.

Baby dragons hatch from their eggs.

The babies hatch a few months later. They dig themselves out of the nest. For the first few years, they mostly live up in the trees. This keeps them safe from **predators**, including other dragons.

In Captivity

In 1927, a Komodo dragon arrived at London Zoo in England. A few years later, a dragon was put on display at the National Zoo in Washington, D.C. But it was difficult to care for the dragons. They did not live for long.

This Komodo dragon lives in a zoo.

This is Auffenberg's assistant, Putra Sastrawan, with a dragon.

Zoos needed to learn more about the dragons and how they lived. In 1969, an American scientist, Walter Auffenberg, moved with his family to Komodo Island. They stayed on the island for nearly a year.

During his stay, Walter Auffenberg caught more than 50 dragons. He studied them carefully. He also wrote a book about them. His work helped zoos to understand how to care for the dragons properly.

A scientist weighs and measures a dragon.

These young
Komodo dragons
were born in a zoo.

There are now dragons in zoos around
the world. Some become tame and
follow their keepers around. In 1992, 13
baby dragons hatched from eggs in the
National Zoo, Washington, D.C. They were
the first dragons born outside Indonesia.

Dragons Today

Today, there are about 4,000 to 5,000 Komodo dragons left in the wild. They face many dangers. Volcanoes and earthquakes destroy their **habitat**. It is also being cleared to make space for farms. Some dragons are killed by **poachers**.

The dragons' habitat is being destroyed.

This is part of the
Komodo National Park.

In 1980, the Komodo National Park was set
up to protect the dragons. The park covers
the islands of Komodo, Rinca, and Padar, and
26 of the smaller islands nearby.

Scientists are still learning more about Komodo dragons. In 2009, a team in Australia took **scans** of a dragon's head. These showed that the dragon might have a **venomous** bite. Before this, people thought that the dragons had venomous spit.

This is Bryan Fry, a scientist who studies Komodo dragons.

The ancestor of the Komodo dragon might have looked like this.

In 2009, scientists found the fossil bones of a giant lizard in Australia. They think that it is the **ancestor** of today's Komodo dragons. It moved from Australia to Indonesia around 900,000 years ago.

Komodo Dragon Timeline

1910

A Dutch soldier leads an expedition to find a Komodo dragon.

1911

The first Komodo dragons in captivity are kept in Bogor Zoo, Java.

1912

Peter Ouwens publishes the first scientific report about the Komodo dragon.

1926

W. Douglas Burden leads an expedition to catch a live Komodo dragon. He brings back two live dragons for the Bronx Zoo, in New York.

1927

Komodo dragons arrive at the London Zoo, in England.

1934

A Komodo dragon arrives at the National Zoo, in Washington, D.C., but it only lives for two years.

1969

Walter Auffenberg spends a year on Komodo Island, studying dragons.

1980

Komodo National Park is set up in Indonesia.

1992

Baby Komodo dragons are born outside Indonesia for the first time at the National Zoo in Washington, D.C.

2009

Scientists discover that the Komodo dragon might have a venomous bite.

2009

Scientists discover that the ancestors of the Komodo dragon might have come from Australia.

Glossary

ancestor family member who lived a very long time ago

bait food used as a trap for catching animals

forked with one end divided into two points

habitat natural place in which a plant or animal lives

monitor lizard kind of large lizard

poacher someone who hunts for animals when it is against the law

predator animal that hunts other animals for food

prey animal that is hunted by another animal for food

reptile cold-blooded animal that breathes air and has a backbone; most reptiles lay eggs and have scaly skin

respect believe in the quality and worth of someone or something

scan picture of the inside of a human or animal's body

serrated with a jagged edge

venomous able to produce a poison called venom and inject it with a bite or sting

Find Out More

Books

Bjorklund, Ruth. *Komodo Dragons* (Nature's Children).
  New York: Children's Press, 2012.

Ganeri, Anita. *Introducing Asia* (Introducing Continents).
  Chicago: Heinemann Library, 2014.

Royston, Angela. *Reptiles* (Animal Classifications).
  Chicago: Heinemann Library, 2015.

Websites

FactHound offers a safe, fun way to find Internet sites related to this book. All of the sites on FactHound have been researched by our staff.

Here's all you do:

Visit www.facthound.com
Type in this code: 9781484627112

Index